Richard Trevithick

The Quiz Book

compiled by

Peter Richardson

edited by

Peter Joseph

Published by The Trevithick Society
for Industrial Archaeology in Cornwall

Copyright © Peter Richardson

British Library Cataloguing Data

Richardson, Peter
Richard Trevithick. The Quiz Book.
1 Engineering - England - Cornwall
1 Title

ISBN 978-0-904040-73-9

All rights reserved. No part of this publication may be reproduced, stored in a retrieval system, or transmitted in any form or by any means, electronic, mechanical, photocopying, recording or otherwise, without the prior permission of the Trevithick Society.

Printed and bound in Cornwall by R. Booth Ltd
Penryn, Cornwall Great Britain, TR10 9HH

Typeset by Peninsula Projects, Penzance, Cornwall

Whilst the Trevithick Society is confident that the author has conducted his research diligently, for he was to be examined on his work in a most public manner, the society cannot accept responsibility for any errors or omissions in the text. Neither can it accept responsibility for any losses or inconvenience whatsoever that might arise from the use of any of the information contained herein.

Dedicated to the Memory of
David Jenkin
a long time Member of the Society

PREFACE

The Trevithick Society was delighted when Peter Richardson made an approach with his proposal to compete in the BBC Mastermind television programme with 'The Life and Works of Richard Trevithick, 1771 – 1833' as his chosen subject.

Trevithick's successful development of the high-pressure steam engine in mining, transport and industry has been generally unknown and unappreciated. For too long his accomplishments against prejudice and commercial interests had been confined to the history books and the hearts of Cornishmen; his fulsome life deserved better recognition. History reveals that he had received a raw deal at the hands of those who made fortunes from his ideas and endeavours.

Trevithick worked at the very limits of technical knowledge, often putting his life at risk to prove his theories. Few could keep pace with him as he discarded friends, family, homeland and valuable patents in a headlong dash to demonstrate more applications for his high-pressure, or 'strong', steam.

Many think that Trevithick's battles with James Watt and beasts in the jungles of South America rate his life's story alongside that of any swashbuckling Caribbean pirate.

Peter Richardson's offer to delve into Trevithick's life and to kindly present his research to the society in the form of hundreds of questions and answers was a proposal that this society, the world of industrial archaeology and the students of Cornwall's rich mining history have welcomed with enthusiasm.

The text has been formatted and illustrated from the society's library by its Curator, Pete Joseph and all has been made possible by a bequest from the estate of the late David Jenkin, a mining man from Camborne and enthusiastic member of this society.

Every child should be aware of the contribution Trevithick made to his country's heritage, the Industrial Revolution and the development of the world. Maybe this book will achieve that dream.

Philip M Hosken
Chairman
The Trevithick Society

ABOUT THE AUTHOR

Peter Richardson was a bright lad at school and started his working life in the research laboratories of Kodak. He returned after three years National Service to work his way through the Kodak Company and take charge of its photo chemicals plant at Kirkby in Merseyside.

Peter first took an interest in quizzing when he joined the Merseyside Quiz Team in 1970. He started media quizzing in 1973 by winning Treble Chance on radio with a Southport team. He continued by playing seventy half-hour games on thirty different programmes. He appeared twice on the Brain of Britain programme and came very close to winning the title each time. He was semi-finalist on Mastermind in 1977 and won Krypton Factor in 1979.

While Peter is not a professional quiz player he has taken the money when it has been offered and is proud of having collected several thousands of pounds by using his remarkable ability to answer questions. His most lucrative adventures were on Sale of the Century and three times in the Australian Sale of a Century programme, he describes these profits as making quizzing a useful hobby.

Peter Richardson is a family man with two daughters who celebrated his golden wedding in 2005. The Trevithick Society is grateful to Peter for his donation of the many weeks of his work that have made this quiz book possible; work that also enabled him to win his round on Mastermind in 2005.

CONTENTS

Preface   iv

About the author   v

Section A: the Questions   pages 1-35

Section B: the Answers   pages 36-70

Young Trevithick

Q1. On what date was Richard Trevithick born?
Q2. Where was Richard Trevithick born?
Q3. In which year were his parents married?
Q4. What were the occupations of his father and uncle in 1760?
Q5. What was Richard Trevithick's mother's maiden name?
Q6. Where did the Teague family came from?
Q7. Where did the family move to in 1771?
Q8. Who now owns the property?
Q9. What was the name of his last sister, born 1773?
Q10. What new type of engine was introduced in 1775 and where?
Q11. What was built at Dolcoath in 1776-7 by Richard Trevithick Senior?
Q12. What was the really big event of 1778?
Q13. What was their unique selling point?
Q14. What did the new engine cut fuel costs to?
Q15. How did this affect Cornish mining?
Q16. How long did it take Boulton and Watt to get a virtual monopoly in Cornwall?
Q17. Why was it so popular in Cornwall?
Q18. What did Boulton and Watt charge for using their engines?
Q19. Who worked out what the savings were?
Q20. What did William Murdoch do in 1784?
Q21. Why did he give the idea up?
Q22. Why did that matter?
Q23. What was his other distinction?
Q24. How did Richard get on at school?
Q25. How did the teacher describe him?
Q26. How many sums did he say he could do to the teacher's one?
Q27. What were his best subjects at school?
Q28. How tall was he?
Q29. What sport did he engage in?
Q30. Which big (6 foot tall) man did he hold upside down and push feet against a count house ceiling?

Q31. On what occasion?
Q32. What weight did he hang from his thumb while signing a beam 6 feet high?
Q33. What did he throw across a yard and over an engine house roof?
Q34. What did he pick up and carry off on his shoulder?
Q35. Which weighed?
Q36. What else did he lift and where did it go?
Q37. Who came to hear of him because of his physique?
Q38. Who made a journey to see him for his physique?
Q39. Who concluded?
Q40. How did he learn engineering?
Q41. What happened to make Boulton and Watt's one-third duty very unpopular?
Q42. What was it called?
Q43. Why did that matter in 1784?
Q44. What was the weakness in Boulton and Watt's patents?
Q45. What was strong steam?
Q46. What were the grounds for Watt's objections?
Q47. Who was the first engineer in Cornwall to attack Watt's patents?
Q48. What did he invent?
Q49. Who wrote to Hornblower in 1791 urging the advantage of strong steam?
Q50. Where and when was Hornblower's first working compound engine erected in Cornwall?
Q51. Where and when did Richard start work?
Q52. What was his next recorded job?
Q53. What was his salary?
Q54. Who else was employed at East Stray Park?
Q55. What was he commissioned for in 1792?
Q56. What did he conclude?
Q57. Which engineer was the next to compete against Boulton and Watt?
Q58. What happened?
Q59. Where did Richard assist Bull in trying another different but illegal engine?
Q60. What did they literally fight off?
Q61. Where were they finally served with their writs?
Q62. Where did Richard re-erect an engine in 1795?
Q63. Who did Richard and Bull work with to build their engines?
Q64. Who was West employed by?

2

Q65. How did West become (tenuously) related to Richard?
Q66. What did Richard make at home in 1797?

Richard Trevithick's birthplace, Station Road, Pool. The engine house in the background is Palmer's Shaft, at South Wheal Crofty.

Richard Trevithick as a young boy. Taken from Francis Trevithick's biography of his father.

Adult Trevithick

Q67. What changed Richard's life in 1797 (aged 26)?
Q68. What did this mean?
Q69. Which were they?
Q70. And?
Q71. What other major change occurred?
Q72. When and where were they married?
Q73. Where did they live at first?
Q74. Where did they go next and when?
Q75. What mistake did Richard Trevithick make when moving?
Q76. Which child was born in Camborne in 1798?
Q77. What was the major development in 1798?
Q78. Did he make any profit from plunger pumps?
Q79. What did he develop from plunger-pumps?
Q80. Where and when was the first one installed?
Q81. Why was his water-powered plunger engine not used much in Cornwall?
Q82. Where did he install them?
Q83. How much did he earn from those?
Q84. Where and when did Richard Trevithick modify a Boulton and Watt engine to accept high-pressure steam?
Q85. What was it used for?
Q86. What other type of engine did Richard Trevithick design in 1798?
Q87. Where was the first one installed?
Q88. What was the crucial point which enabled high-pressure working?
Q89. Whose advice did he seek on this point?
Q90. What was the advice he got?
Q91. Where did he build his models of these puffer engines in?
Q92. Who made the models for him?
Q93. Who 'stoked' the boiler?
Q94. Who turned the steam on to set it going?
Q95. What steam pressure was used in the practical puffer engines?
Q96. Where did the excess steam go?
Q97. What did he do with the very hot blast-pipe?

Q98. Where and when did Richard Trevithick install the first puffer engine?
Q99. How many were erected in first four years?
Q100. What did one for Wheal Margaret cost the owner, Mr. Millet?
Q101. What did Boulton and Watt propose in an attempt to stop the puffer engine success?
Q102. Finally carried out where?
Q103. How much did Richard Trevithick bet that his engine would win?
Q104. Who took up the challenge and looked after the Boulton and Watt engine?
Q105. What had he been up to?
Q106. How may he have sabotaged Richard Trevithick's engine?
Q107. How was the trial conducted?
Q108. What was the outcome?
Q109. What, dating from 1803-4, can be seen in the Science Museum?
Q110. What event of 1800 pleased Cornish engineers?
Q111. Which engineering works was founded in 1801?

The Camborne Road Carriage

Q112. Who built the world's first steam road vehicle, and when?
Q113. What were the main defects of the Cugnot machine?
Q114. What was the fate of the Cugnot engine after its trials?
Q115. Who was the second inventor with a claim to the steam carriage?
Q116. Who did he work for?
Q117. What was the attitude of Boulton and Watt?
Q118. How many good working models had Murdoch made by 1795?
Q119. Where?
Q120. Who saw and discussed the models in Murdoch's house?
Q121. What major advance, not in the Watt Patents, had Murdoch made?
Q122. Why did Murdoch give up?
Q123. What did that mean in terms of priority?
Q124. What did Murdoch go on to do that made him wealthy?
Q125. What was the first step for Richard Trevithick before building road carriage?
Q126. What experiment did he make?
Q127. Who had previously hired the chaise?
Q128. Where were the cylinder and boiler cast?
Q129. Who assembled it?
Q130. Where?
Q131. Whose workshop did the finer work?
Q132. When was the first run?
Q133. Where did tradition say she went?
Q134. Where did she actually go?
Q135. How did old Stephen Williams describe it?
Q136. How fast did she go?
Q137. What did Richard Trevithick agree with Andrew Vivian?
Q138. How did it end?
Q139. What important event was this?
Q140. What then?
Q141. What did it cost, not counting their labour?
Q142. What was its nickname?
Q143. How was it commemorated in 2001?

Q144. What did Davies Giddy inspect at Marazion in November 1801?
Q145. What did he spot?
Q146. How should future boilers be built?
Q147. How were they cast?

The Trevithick Society's full-scale working replica of the Puffing Devil.

Photograph copyright of Phil Monkton, Cornwall and Isles of Scilly Press.

The next step - London!

Q148. What was Richard Trevithick and Andrew Vivian's first step, completed in 1802?
Q149. For what purposes?
Q150. Who held the patent?
Q151. Who gave them letters of introduction?
Q152. Which two notable scientists did they meet?
Q153. On what date was the patent granted?
Q154. What did they omit from the patent that was worth a fortune?
Q155. How did the London Carriage differ from the Camborne prototype?
Q156. Where were the parts built and by whom?
Q157. Where were they assembled?
Q158. How big was it?
Q159. How big were the wheels?
Q160. What was the minor but damaging fault?
Q161. How fast did it go?
Q162. Provided that?
Q163. What was its performance like on hills?
Q164. Which part of London was it driven round?
Q165. Which road was closed for a special trial to take place?
Q166. What nickname was the engine given?
Q167. How many orders were placed?
Q168. Where did the engine finish up?
Q169. Why did it not catch on?
Q170. What gearing fault did it have?
Q171. What advantages did it have over horses?
Q172. What was the major problem with horses?

More about 1802 - 1804: trains

Q173. What sort of pressures was Richard Trevithick working with in trials?
Q174. Where and when did he write that statement?
Q175. What may he have done, or started, at Coalbrookdale in 1803?
Q176. Who was in charge at Coalbrookdale then?
Q177. What idea is he known to have?
Q178. What does this imply?
Q179. What evidence is there of this?
Q180. What disaster set back the acceptance of Richard Trevithick's engines in 1803?
Q181. On what date?
Q182. What casualties were there?
Q183. What was the size of boiler?
Q184. How heavy was the largest fragment flung and what did it weigh?
Q185. What caused this explosion?
Q186. What else happened?
Q187. How were future engines to be modified?
Q188. What else resulted from the explosion?

The Penydarren Locomotive

Q189. When did Richard Trevithick get the first approach?
Q190. Who contacted him?
Q191. What did he want to discuss?
Q192. How many ironworks were there in the area?
Q193. What had they banded together to build?
Q194. For what purpose was it built?
Q195. What was the serious problem with the canal?
Q196. What was the most congested stretch?
Q197. What did they build along this stretch?
Q198. What was this for?
Q199. What was the shape of rails?
Q200. What sort of wheels were to run on them?
Q201. What was the gauge?
Q202. What did Richard Trevithick propose to Homfray?
Q203. Who did not like Homfray and dismissed the idea of a locomotive?
Q204. What was his principal objection?
Q205. What was the big wager?
Q206. What else?
Q207. What distance was that?
Q208. Why the 10 ton weight?
Q209. Who was the stakeholder and referee?
Q210. Where was the engine built?
Q211. What type of boiler did the engine have?
Q212. How was the smoke exhausted?
Q213. What was the size of the cylinder?
Q214. How did the drive operate?
Q215. Why was the drive only one side?
Q216. Why use a flywheel?
Q217. Which engineer was coming down from London to see the engine?
Q218. Who did he work for?
Q219. What was the date of the famous run?
Q220. What load was carried?
Q221. What was the total weight?

Q222. How fast did she go?
Q223. How long did it take?
Q224. Why so long?
Q225. How much fuel did it use?
Q226. What went wrong on the return journey?
Q227. What did Crawshay say?
Q228. How did he and Hill try to wriggle out of paying?
Q229. What minor mishap occurred to Homfray?
Q230. What fatal problem appeared?
Q231. What happened to the engine?
Q232. Who was the next order from?
Q233. Who was John Steel?
Q234. This was unsuccessful because?
Q235. What did Blackett do?
Q236. When did he ask Richard Trevithick to supply another engine to run on them?
Q237. What was Richard Trevithick's reply?
Q238. Who did Richard Trevithick meet while engaged at Wylam in 1805?

Trevithick returns to London

Q239. What major project did Richard Trevithick take on in 1807?
Q240. A tunnel from where to where?
Q241. For which company?
Q242. What was his fee?
Q243. When did the Tunnel Company start work on it?
Q244. Who was the first engineer employed by the Tunnel Company?
Q245. Where did Vazie come from?
Q246. What happened to Vazie's attempt?
Q247. How much money was lost?
Q248. Who gave advice to the Tunnel Company?
Q249. How did Richard Trevithick tackle the job?
Q250. What did he do next and when?
Q251. What was the distance to be covered?
Q252. What were the dimensions of the drift?
Q253. What did Richard Trevithick install as a precaution in September?
Q254. What was the result of problems slowing progress in October?
Q255. How far had they got by this date?
Q256. What was the problem after the excellent progress during November?
Q257. Why were explosives not used?
Q258. Seeing that the job was going to be bigger than he had thought, who did Richard Trevithick bring in?
Q259. Where did the live at first?
Q260. Jane was very unhappy, about what especially?
Q261. How far had they got by January 26th?
Q262. What incident nearly ended the project?
Q263. What day did this happen on?
Q264. Who was the last man out?
Q265. What did some of the directors try to do when progress stalled after the flooding?
Q266. Who upheld the work quality?
Q267. What was required before work was resumed?
Q268. How far had they got by February 4th?

Q269. How long did Richard Trevithick tell Giddy it would be before the holed out?
Q270. What did Richard Trevithick tell the board on Feb 4th?
Q271. What did the Board do?
Q272. What did they conclude?
Q273. What was the Board's reaction?
Q274. What was their last decision?
Q275. What was Richard Trevithick's final advice?
Q276. What happened to the tunnel project?
Q277. How long was it before a tunnel was built using Richard Trevithick's proposed method?
Q278. Where did it happen?
Q279. How long was it before another Thames tunnel was started?
Q280. And how long before it was finished?
Q281. Who started the successful tunnel?
Q282. Who was he assisted by?
Q283. What similarity was there between him and Trevithick?
Q284. Where had Jane and the family moved to?

Ticket for a ride on Catch-Me-Who-Can.

Catch-me-who-can

Q285. What was Richard Trevithick's last attempt to interest London investors in steam transport?
Q286. What is a pure locomotive?
Q287. What step, that George Stephenson took, did he never try?
Q288. So what did he build?
Q289. Where was it built?
Q290. What simpler design did the locomotive engine have?
Q291. What publicity gimmick was used?
Q292. What was the unique selling point?
Q293. Did it work?
Q294. What was the next step?
Q295. What new idea was used on the track?
Q296. What problem reappeared?
Q297. What was the solution?
Q298. What was the public offered?
Q299. Who thought up the name?
Q300. What did Giddy change his name to in 1817?
Q301. Where did the name come from?
Q302. What position would Gilbert hold between 1827 and 1830?
Q303. What other connection was there between Gilbert and Trevithick?
Q304. Gilbert attended Penzance Grammar School: what other famous scientist was a student there?
Q305. What slogan appeared on the ticket?
Q306. How fast did it go?
Q307. How fast did Richard Trevithick say it would go on a straight line?
Q308. What were the shillings to do?
Q309. How long did it run?
Q310. What brought it all to a close?
Q311. Why couldn't Richard Trevithick put it back together?
Q312. What happened to the engine?
Q313. How many orders or potential investors?

The Catch-Me-Who-Can circuit near the site of Euston Station.

The rest of the London adventures: 1802 - 1811

Q314. What did the Government ask him about in 1803?
Q315. Who approached him?
Q316. Where did they meet?
Q317. What did Stafford ask Richard Trevithick to do?
Q318. What happened?
Q319. How did it end?
Q320. What experiment did Richard Trevithick make as a result?
Q321. What was the design?
Q322. What was the result?
Q323. Which American built a similar vessel about the same time and did well?

Dredging

Q324. Which bucket-dredging enthusiast ordered a Richard Trevithick engine in 1803?
Q325. Why was that order cancelled in September?
Q326. How many dredgers did Richard Trevithick have on the Thames in 1806-7?
Q327. What were they mounted on?
Q328. What contract was Richard Trevithick after?
Q329. What had he never done before – a serious weakness?
Q330. What did he find he needed?
Q331. What did that do to his costs?
Q332. Where did his dredgers work?
Q333. Where else did they work?
Q334. What else in East India Dock at Blackwall?

The Dickinson disaster

Q335. Who was Dickinson?
Q336. What else did Dickinson do?
Q337. How many patents did he take out 1802-26?
Q338. What was the first Richard Trevithick Robert Dickinson patent and when?
Q339. What was the Nautical Labourer?
Q340. What had Richard Trevithick tried to do in 1804?
Q341. What stopped him?
Q342. What did they achieve with the 1808 patent?
Q343. The second Richard Trevithick Robert Dickinson patent?
Q344. What was their partnership set up to do?
Q345. Where?
Q346. What were the original uses?
Q347. What other use?
Q348. What was the next use of iron barrels?
Q349. Where and when did Richard Trevithick raise his first wreck?
Q350. How did he manage it?
Q351. What problem had he not expected?
Q352. What problem did he encounter when the wreck was raised?
Q353. How did Richard Trevithick resolve the dispute?
Q354. What did he get paid for his efforts?
Q355. Did he ever raise another wreck in England?
Q356. What was Dickinson complaining about vigorously?
Q357. What did they do in 1809?
Q358. What did it cover?
Q359. Which was the only one ever put on the market by them?
Q360. What ended it all in 1810?
Q361. Which developed into?
Q362. Who sent for the doctors?
Q363. Who advised Jane to bring him home?
Q364. When was he well enough to return home?
Q365. How did he leave London?
Q366. Accompanied by?

Q367. How long was the first leg of the voyage?
Q368. Why was an escort necessary?
Q369. What did Richard Trevithick do in Dover?
Q370. After the Falmouth Packet left Dover?
Q371. How long was the voyage to Falmouth?
Q372. How far is it from Falmouth to Camborne?
Q373. How did Richard Trevithick and son Richard do that trip?
Q374. What more bad news awaited him at Penponds?

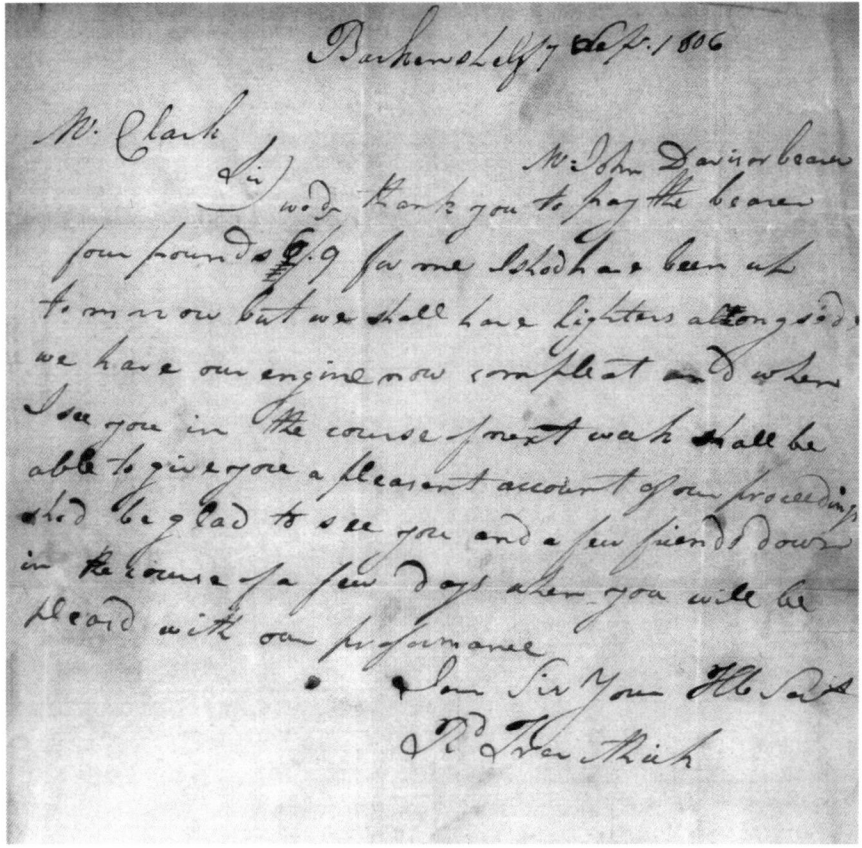

Letter written by Richard Trevithick in 1806, just before he commenced work on the Thames Tunnel.

Trevithick Society Archive

Back home

Q375. What major disaster befell Richard Trevithick on 11 February 1811?
Q376. How did he raise money?
Q377. What did Bankruptcy Court find?
Q378. What were Richard Trevithick's assets?
Q379. How much did Richard Trevithick eventually pay off?
Q380. What was Dickinson's contribution?
Q381. What was the result of the Bankruptcy Court hearing?
Q382. What is a sponging house?
Q383. Why was there a delay in granting a certificate of release?
Q384. What papers were these?
Q385. What date was Richard Trevithick's discharge finally granted on?
Q386. What important event happened in the spring of 1812?
Q387. Define 'Cornish' engine
Q388. What was the unique selling point of this type of engine?
Q389. How expansively?
Q390. What was installed for the first time at Dolcoath Mine in 1812?
Q391. Define 'Cornish' boiler.
Q392. How big was the Dolcoath boiler?
Q393. What was the average duty of the engine using the old and new boilers?
Q394. With whom were boiler orders to be placed?
Q395. What was the first agricultural venture?
Q396. Who was it built for?
Q397. What was it used for?
Q398. Where is it now?
Q399. Who bought the second one, immediately?
Q400. What was the cost effectiveness of the new machine?
Q401. What was the weight and cost of Richard Trevithick's agricultural engines?
Q402. Which independent engine reporting authority appeared with effect from 1811?
Q403. What were his findings?

Q404. Where did Richard Trevithick go during this time?
Q405. How did the bankrupt Richard Trevithick start off the patent for the single-acting expansive engine in 1814?
Q406. What other engine was first installed in Wheal Prosper in 1812?
Q407. Where was the finest and last of them installed in 1815?
Q408. Who was it built by?
Q409. Who was annoyed by this?
Q410. What was John Rastrick doing that distracted his work with the engine?
Q411. With the result that?
Q412. What did Vivian do?
Q413. How did Richard Trevithick personally get it running in January 1816?
Q414. Who designed the Wye Bridge that distracted John Rastrick so much?
Q415. Who was at the door?
Q416. What was the duty, as measured by Gilbert?
Q417. What naval experiment took place in 1813?
Q418. What happened on August 9 1813?
Q419. What was the result?
Q420. What did she go on to do?
Q421. What was her tragic end?

More about John Rastrick

Q422. Which places did John Rastrick visit on his trip in 1812?
Q423. Which engineer was he not impressed by?
Q424. What did he immediately grasp the value of?
Q425. What did he take Richard Trevithick to see?
Q426. What did Rastrick think of it?
Q427. What did they both see?
Q428. What did Richard Trevithick do?
Q429. What was the engineer's name?
Q430. What did the drilling machine do for his costs?
Q431. What was the best result of all?

South America

Q432. Which partnership was started in Lima in 1811?
Q433. What were their origins?
Q434. What was their objective?
Q435. What was their first step?
Q436. What was their advice?
Q437. What did Uvillé find in London on his way home?
Q438. Where?
Q439. What did Uvillé pay for the model?
Q440. What did he do with it?
Q441. When was the new company set up and contracts taken out with the silver mine owners?
Q442. What was their capital?
Q443. What was Uvillé's mission?
Q444. How much money did he have?
Q445. What else was required?
Q446. What was he expressly forbidden to?
Q447. What happened to Uvillé on his voyage round Cape Horn?
Q448. What did he sail on after he recovered?
Q449. Who was one of the passengers?
Q450. When did he finally land?
Q451. What important knowledge did he have?
Q452. What happened first?
Q453. What was his first move?
Q454. What had Richard Trevithick done by 20th May 1813?
Q455. What sort of engines?
Q456. What were the special requirements?
Q457. Why was this necessary?
Q458. How narrow was the track in tight places?
Q459. How urgent was the order?
Q460. Ultimately, what went?
Q461. What else went?
Q462. What did it all cost?
Q463. How much was Uvillé authorised to spend?

Q464. What did Uvillé do?
Q465. What did this entitle him to?
Q466. Was Uvillé empowered to do this?
Q467. Which men were recruited to go with the engines?
Q468. Which relative also went?
Q469. What was Uvillé specifically warned?
Q470. When did they sail, and in what?
Q471. What minor irritation got Uvillé arrested?
Q472. Was this true?
Q473. When did they reach Callao?
Q474. When did they finish unloading?
Q475. Why did some engines eventually work well but others failed?
Q476. What was the principal problem?
Q477. What was Richard Trevithick's solution?

Richard Trevithick in Peru

Q478. What did Richard Trevithick do with his family before leaving for Peru?
Q479. Why did he do this?
Q480. How did he raise money?
Q481. What else did he sell?
Q482. What did he advise any purchaser to?
Q483. What caveat did Richard Trevithick add?
Q484. What did he believe would provide for his family?
Q485. Who did he take with him?
Q486. Why Page?
Q487. When did they sail?
Q488. When did they arrive?
Q489. What did he find?
Q490. What was the situation regarding the engines?
Q491. What else happened on May 19th?
Q492. What was the problem with the waterway which fed the Mint engine?
Q493. Why was this a problem?
Q494. How did Richard Trevithick solve the problem?
Q495. What did Uvillé try to arrange for Richard Trevithick on his way to the mines?
Q496. Why?
Q497. What actually happened?
Q498. What happened after Richard Trevithick had got the engines going properly?
Q499. What did Richard Trevithick do?
Q500. Who tried to keep him?
Q501. What was Richard Trevithick's response?
Q502. What did he do instead?
Q503. What was the result?
Q504. What was the exception?
Q505. What did he take from there?
Q506. When was this lost?

Q507. All was for the best until what happened?
Q508. What revolution?
Q509. Who led the revolution?
Q510. And which British aristocrat?
Q511. How was Cochrane connected with William Murdoch?
Q512. How may Murdoch have benefited from this?
Q513. What was Cochrane doing in 1819?
Q514. What happened at the mine?
Q515. How did Richard Trevithick react?
Q516. Then what happened?
Q517. What did this result in?
Q518. What happened to the mine equipment?
Q519. What happened to Trevithick himself?
Q520. What did Richard Trevithick invent for Bolivar?
Q521. What medical feat did Richard Trevithick achieve after the war?
Q522. What nautical success did Richard Trevithick have in 1822?
Q523. What did he get from the frigate?
Q524. How did he work on the wreck?
Q525. What was he advised to do?

Trevithick's last years in South America

Q526. What did Richard Trevithick actually do with the £2500?
Q527. What was he supposed to be doing?
Q528. How did he plan to revolutionise pearl fishing?
Q529. So what went wrong?
Q530. Who did he meet in Guayaquil?
Q531. Who was James Gerrard?
Q532. What had Gerard learned in 1821?
Q533. What did Gerard find in 1822?
Q534. What was the advantage of this technique?
Q535. Where was the gold?
Q536. So Richard Trevithick and James Gerrard set about in 1822?
Q537. How long did they spend in Costa Rica?
Q538. What did Richard Trevithick and James Gerrard find in Costa Rica?
Q539. What did Richard Trevithick report to the Costa Rican government in March 1824?
Q540. What did Trevithick and Gerrard decide to do in 1826?
Q541. Which way did they decide to go home?
Q542. What were their reasons?
Q543. How far was it from the mines to Puerte de San Juan?
Q544. How many set out on the journey?
Q545. How long did it take them to reach San Juan del Norte?
Q546. How did they get there?
Q547. Had it ever been done before?
Q548. What was the first very serious problem?
Q549. Which way did they go?
Q550. What did they find when they got off the ridge?
Q551. What did this result in?
Q552. How did they manage the next stage?
Q553. What did they decide to do?
Q554. What happened to the raft?
Q555. What happened to the raft's occupants?
Q556. How did the cross the river?

Q557. Was this successful?
Q558. Who helped him?
Q559. Where did things improve?
Q560. How did they reach Puerte San Juan?
Q561. What did Richard Trevithick think of the route?

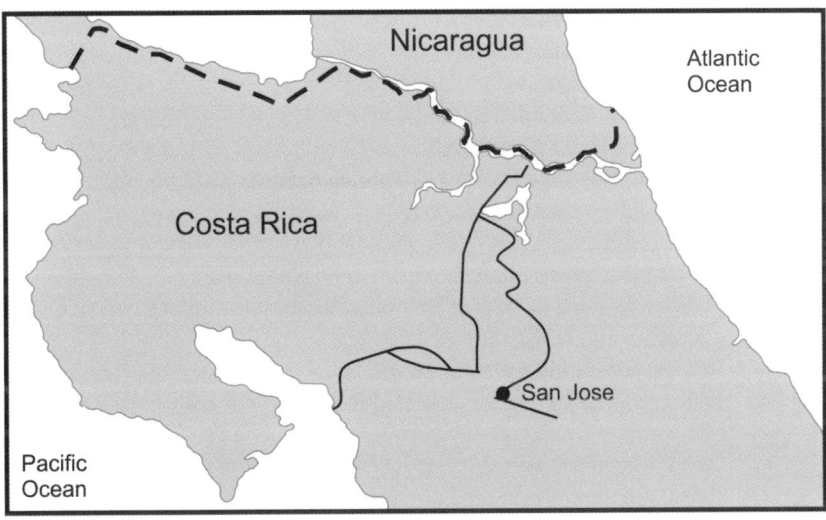

The routes taken by Richard Trevithick across northern Costa Rica.

Escape from South America

Q562. Where did they go next?
Q563. How did they get from San Juan to Cartagena?
Q564. What did possessions did they have left?
Q565. How far is it?
Q566. Where did Richard Trevithick have another brush with death on the journey to Cartagena?
Q567. What happened?
Q568. What did that result in?
Q569. Who saved him?
Q570. What did he do?
Q571. What condition was Trevithick in?
Q572. What was Hall doing there?
Q573. Who did Hall take Richard Trevithick to meet in Cartagena?
Q574. What did Stephenson give him?
Q575. How did Richard Trevithick get home?
Q576. What possessions did he have when he got home?
Q577. What happened to Gerard and the schoolboys?
Q578. What adventure did they have?
Q579. Which school did the boys go to?
Q580. Where did Jose Maria Montelegre, one of the schoolboys, go on to?
Q581. What did he become in 1860?
Q582. What money-making idea did they take home?

Jane Trevithick

Q583. Where had Richard Trevithick left Jane and the children?
Q584. Where was Richard (III) working in 1819?
Q585. What job did he have?
Q586. What was the Cornish Copper Company's attitude?
Q587. What did they do?
Q588. Which of Richard Trevithick's sons was taken on next at Hayle?
Q589. What did he become?
Q590. What battle was Jane losing?
Q591. Which were?
Q592. Who was the patent taken up by?
Q593. Who was Richard Trevithick's solicitor and what did he find?
Q594. What was happening on these mines?
Q595. Who took up the case for Jane?
Q596. How did they get on?
Q597. Some savings were paid; what were they due to?
Q598. What was the problem there?
Q599. What did Henry do for Jane in 1824?
Q600. Where is it?
Q601. What was her job?
Q602. How long did she stay there?
Q603. When did she die?
Q604. In due course, who else did Henry take on at the Hayle Foundry?
Q605. What post did Francis the biographer hold eventually?
Q606. And where did two of the sons go?

Richard Trevithick's last years in Cornwall

Q607. On arriving back in Cornwall, where did Richard Trevithick find his family?
Q608. What was Jane doing?
Q609. What were the savings from Trevithick's inventions calculated to be?
Q610. What did he get as final payment from the two faithful mines?
Q611. Which were they?
Q612. What opinion of Trevithick was expressed by Williams of the United Mines in 1853?
Q613. Did United Mines pay any more in the 1820s?
Q614. What patent was still unfinished in 1827?
Q615. What happened to that idea?
Q616. Who was it considered by?
Q617. They reported?
Q618. What idea was aired with Gilbert on June 29th 1828?
Q619. What was under construction at Hayle 1828?
Q620. Which acquaintance from Lima did Richard Trevithick write to about the gun and the iron ship?
Q621. With what result?
Q622. How much did Trevithick and Gerard raise in England for their Costa Rica shares?
Q623. What was the one offer?
Q624. What was his reaction?
Q625. What did Gerard do?
Q626. Who was the petition for a pension for Trevithick presented to Parliament by?
Q627. When was this?
Q628. In what capacity?
Q629. What was the claim that he repeated?
Q630. Who was the claim strongly supported by?
Q631. What was the result?
Q632. What foreign invitation did Richard Trevithick receive in July 1828?

Q633. Why him?
Q634. How did he raise the fare?
Q635. Who did he give 5s of it to?
Q636. What did he find?
Q637. What did Richard Trevithick do in Holland?
Q638. What did Richard Trevithick do back in England?
Q639. When was it ready for trial?
Q640. How did it perform on test for the Board?
Q641. What was the duty on the engine?
Q642. How was it to be conveyed?
Q643. What prevented the pump being used?
Q644. What was the row about?
Q645. What was his next idea conceived in 1829?
Q646. Who was it built by?
Q647. What was his conclusion?
Q648. What did he decide?
Q649. What was the last idea of 1829?
Q650. Where were such engines used?
Q651. Which likely customers never took to them?
Q652. What was the final Cornish disaster, in 1830?
Q653. What was the result?
Q654. What did his family do?
Q655. What had Richard Trevithick done for Harvey?
Q656. Why was this necessary?
Q657. What was Richard Trevithick expected to do?
Q658. What did he threaten to do when Harvey wrote to him in London?
Q659. What did he do in the end?

The final years in London

Q660. Where did Richard Trevithick live, for choice?
Q661. Why here in particular?
Q662. What had he done for Davies Gilbert earlier?
Q663. What was this idea?
Q664. What was the storage heater full of?
Q665. How was it used?
Q666. Did it catch on?
Q667. What was Richard Trevithick's last patent in 1832?
Q668. Who did he join to experiment with it?
Q669. What type of industry did Hall's company become involved in?
Q670. What did Richard Trevithick design for Hall which was profitable?
Q671. Where did Richard Trevithick stay while he was in Dartford?
Q672. What was Richard Trevithick's final idea?
Q673. To be built to celebrate what?
Q674. What reform was this?
Q675. What was it to be made of?
Q676. What would the weight have been?
Q677. What was it to be topped by?
Q678. How were people to get up and down it?
Q679. What were the diameters at bottom and top?
Q680. How big was the platform at the top?
Q681. The high was the statue to be?
Q682. What finish was the tower to have?
Q683. Who did he write to for support?
Q684. When was an acknowledgement received?
Q685. When did Richard Trevithick die?
Q686. Where did Richard Trevithick die?
Q687. Who buried him?
Q688. Who paid for the funeral?
Q689. Where did the funeral take place?
Q690. Why not the Parish Churchyard?
Q691. Why was this ironic?
Q692. Who told the family?

Q693. What was the family's reaction?
Q694. And finally, what did Richard Trevithick say about himself?

Engraving of Richard Trevithick, taken from Francis Trevithick's biography.

Photogrpah of Jane Trevithick, date unknown.

A685. On April 22nd 1833, after a week's illness in bed.
A686. At the Bull Inn, Dartford,
A687. Hall's workmen carried him to the grave and mounted a guard to keep off body snatchers.
A688. Hall's workmen are said to have collected the money to pay the expenses but Hall himself probably did that.
A689. The chapel of St. Edmund, King and martyr, Dartford.
A690. It was too low-lying and the ground too damp for graves.
A691. Steam pumping would have drained the area!
A692. Rowley Potter, a Dartford tradesman.
A693. Nothing is recorded.
A694. Branded with folly and madness for attempting what the world calls impossibilities. This has so far been my reward from the public, but should this be all, I should be satisfied by the great secret pleasure and laudable pride that I feel in my own breast from having been the instrument of bringing forward new principles and new arrangements of boundless value to my country, and however much I may be straitened in pecuniary circumstances, the great honour of being a useful subject can never be taken from me, which far exceeds riches."

The final years in London

A660. Lauderdale House, Highgate.
A661. His health was beginning to go and he was happier in the clean air on a hill.
A662. Fitted his house with steam heating.
A663. A house warming storage heater.
A664. Steam heated hot water.
A665. It was wheeled about the house covered with a movable skirt to regulate heat release.
A666. Yes, quite a few were made by John Hall, prized, not hidden. The patents were profitable.
A667. A complex steam engine with a multitubular boiler using superheated steam, with a heat exchanger and condenser.
A668. John Hall of Dartford.
A669. Refrigeration.
A670. A range of boilers producing up to 150 pounds per square inch steam. Hall made and sold quite a lot of these.
A671. The Bull in Dartford; Going up to Highgate as often as possible.
A672. The Reform Tower.
A673. The Reform Act of 1832.
A674. Parliament! "To take effectual Measures for correcting diverse Abuses that have long prevailed in the Choice of Members to serve in the Commons House of Parliament."
A675. 1,500 10-foot square cast iron plates stacking up to 1000ft high
A676. 6,000 tons.
A677. A statue.
A678. Using a passenger lift driven by steam-compressed air to a gallery at the top.
A679. 100 feet and 12 feet.
A680. 50ft diameter.
A681. 40 feet.
A682. Gilded!
A683. William IV.
A684. March 1st 1833.

A633.	Probably because his nephew Nicholas was an engineer to the Steam Navigation Company in Rotterdam.
A634.	He borrowed £2 from a neighbour and relative, John Tyzack.
A635.	A beggar who said his pig had died.
A636.	That Holland was sinking; that drainage was getting beyond windmills.
A637.	He joined the Steam Navigation Company and proposed using six engines for pumping.
A638.	He got Harvey's Foundry to make a ball and chain pump 3 feet in diameter with a high-pressure steam pump.
A639.	July 1829.
A640.	It lifted 7,200 gallons of water 10 feet in a minute, using one bushel of coals an hour.
A641.	34.5 millions, exceeding good for so small an engine.
A642.	All in an iron barge.
A643.	After the directors left for refreshment, well satisfied, a row broke out, the Board stamped off, and the device never left Hayle.
A644.	Nobody knows, but Trevithick's hot temper had wrecked his prospects once again.
A645.	The closed cycle engine, driven by superheated steam with the partially condensed steam fed back to boiler.
A646.	John Brunton, an apprentice,
A647.	He saw that it would not work.
A648.	That he dare not tell Trevithick.
A649.	Portable puffer engines on ships for loading, unloading, warping, pumping and, possibly, cooking.
A650.	On fishing boats for hauling the nets in and for raising sails on huge sailing steamers.
A651.	London Colliers.
A652.	Furious row with Harvey.
A653.	He stormed off and went to London.
A654.	They stayed in Hayle with Henry Harvey.
A655.	He had studied and modelled the Hayle harbour and its three rivers.
A656.	To clarify a court case against the Copperhouse Foundry for building sluices which had altered the course of the Penpol River and removed some of Harvey's land.
A657.	Appear as a witness for Harvey.
A658.	Appear for Copperhouse.
A659.	He turned up and gave his evidence for Harvey, but he did not go home to Cornwall.

Richard Trevithick's last years in Cornwall

A607. In Hayle, being supported by Henry Harvey.
A608. Still managing Henry's company hotel, the White Hart.
A609. Over half a million pounds.
A610. £150.
A611. Treskerby and Wheal Chance.
A612. "I have often expressed my opinion that he was at the same time the greatest and the worst-used man in Cornwall."
A613. No.
A614. A recoil gun mounting.
A615. Gerard took it to the Admiralty; it died.
A616. The Select Committee of Artillery Officers, later The Ordnance Board.
A617. "That on examination of the invention they consider it to be wholly inapplicable to practical purposes."
A618. Refrigeration by expansion of chilled compressed air.
A619. An iron ship; it was never finished.
A620. Lord Cochrane.
A621. Trevithick did not receive an answer.
A622. Nothing.
A623. £8,000 for the whole of Richard Trevithick's share.
A624. "I'd rather kick him downstairs".
A625. He went to Holland and France, raised no interest, and died penniless in Paris in 1830.
A626. Davies Gilbert.
A627. 27 February 1828.
A628. Gilbert was Member of Parliament for Bodmin.
A629. That Trevithick had saved Cornwall more than half a million and listed all his other inventions.
A630. The Cornish mine owners, the same people who refused to pay his allowances.
A631. Not a penny.
A632. To go to Holland to look at vessels on the Rhine and to see the drainage problems.

Jane Trevithick

A583. Penzance.
A584. At uncle Henry Harvey's foundry for £30/year.
A585. Trying to improve access to Hayle harbour by dredging the River Penpol.
A586. Hostile.
A587. Hired gangs to shovel dredging spoil back into the river at night.
A588. John Harvey Trevithick.
A589. Merchant and shipowner,
A590. Collecting dues for plunger pole engines.
A591. One quarter of all savings above duty of 26M.
A592. William Sims, acting for Michael Williams of United Mines.
A593. Richard Edmonds; he found that only two mines were paying the allowance.
A594. They were under attack from some of their shareholders for paying the allowance.
A595. Henry Harvey and Davies Gilbert.
A596. They failed.
A597. The Cornish boiler.
A598. Richard Trevithick had not patented it.
A599. He installed her (with her younger sons) as landlady of the White Hart hotel.
A600. In Foundry Square, Hayle.
A601. Entertaining and putting up company guests.
A602. Until 1836, when she was 64.
A603. In 1868, aged 96.
A604. Francis (Richard's biographer) and Frederick.
A605. Loco Superintendent of London and NW railway.
A606. To Japan; some of their direct descendants are still there and are very proud of their ancestry.

Escape from South America

A562. Cartagena in Colombia.
A563. No one knows; along the coast somehow.
A564. What they stood up in.
A565. Five or six hundred miles!
A566. On the Magdalena estuary.
A567. He upset a black man who retaliated by capsizing his canoe.
A568. Almost drowning and with an alligator advancing on him.
A569. Bruce Napier Hall, who was shooting wild pigs on the bank, who heard Richard Trevithick call for help.
A570. Shot the alligator in the eye and made a lasso and pulled Richard Trevithick to the bank.
A571. "Half starved, half hanged, and the rest devoured by alligators".
A572. He was an officer in the Venezuelan Service.
A573. Robert Stephenson (son of George).
A574. £50 to get him home.
A575. From Cartagena to Jamaica, then by packet to Falmouth, landing 12 October 1827.
A576. His clothes, his gold watch, a drawing compass, a magnetic compass and a pair of silver spurs.
A577. They went with Stephenson to the United States in the brig Bunker Hill.
A578. The brig was wrecked with no loss of life; they went on to Niagara Falls, then from New York to Liverpool, arriving November 11th 1827.
A579. The 'Gents Boarding Academy', Lauderdale House, Highgate.
A580. The Royal College of Medicine in Edinburgh.
A581. The President of Costa Rica.
A582. Growing coffee! Europeans could not get enough of it.

A549. Between the volcanoes of Poas (rather active then and now) and Barva to the headwaters of a tributary of the Serapique.
A550. Soft, swampy ground.
A551. They sent back the three labourers and the mules.
A552. By following streams they got to the Serapique. But travelling along its banks was very hard.
A553. They built a raft.
A554. It fetched up against an impassable fallen tree in some rapids.
A555. Trevithick and two men were on one bank and the rest of the party on the other.
A556. They decided to swim.
A557. The first man got across but the second was swept away and drowned; Richard Trevithick only just made it.
A558. Gerard, by throwing him a creeper.
A559. Where the river became navigable at Puerto Viejo.
A560. Without too much trouble, using rafts and canoes.
A561. That it would be quite easy to build a mule track from PuertoViejo to the mines!

Jane Trevithick with members of her family, presumably some of her and Richard's children.

The last years in South America

A526. He bought a ship, the *Devan*, and sailed off to Costa Rica to go pearl-fishing.
A527. Running an errand for Bolivar to Bogota.
A528. Use a diving bell as he had on the San Martin.
A529. He could not wring permission from the Costa Rican bureaucracy.
A530. James A. Gerard.
A531. A Scottish trader working the Pacific coast of South America.
A532. That gold mines were being opened up by a priest named Castro.
A533. A local man called Alverado extracting gold from ore by amalgamation with mercury, which is then boiled off.
A534. It saved the cost of transporting ore across mountains.
A535. At Monte del Aguacata, maybe 5,000ft high.
A536. Prospecting for gold.
A537. Four years,
A538. The mines of Quebrada-Honda and Coralillo.
A539. That there was much gold and silver and that he could mine it easily with the right equipment and labour.
A540. Go home to raise a lot of capital and come back well supported.
A541. From the Atlantic coast rather than the Pacific.
A542. They wanted to avoid the Horn and prove that the much better harbour at Puerte de San Juan was accessible from the mines, making for much lower transport costs to and from Europe.
A543. 60 miles.
A544. Eleven: Richard Trevithick and James Gerrard with his servant; three labourers to go all the way and three to go as far as the River Serapique; and José Maria and Mariano Montelegre, schoolboys going to England for an education!
A545. Three weeks.
A546. Through the Cordilleras to the River Serapiqui, down that to the River San Juan, and to its mouth.
A547. No, they were the first white men to cross the Isthmus of Nicaragua.
A548. The usable routes through and off the Cordilleras were very hard to find.

A503.	He found plenty; mostly it was too remote to develop with the capital available to him.
A504.	One mine with copper and silver in Caxatambo, in Chile.
A505.	£5,000 worth of ore.
A506.	When the Spaniards recaptured the area in the fighting and Richard Trevithick had to run.
A507.	The Revolution reached Lima and Peru.
A508.	Against the government by Old Spain with a Viceroy.
A509.	Simon Bolivar, Bernado O'Higgins, and Jose de San Martin.
A510.	Sir Thomas ('Tommy') Cochrane; Admiral of the Chilean navy.
A511.	Murdoch, as a friend of Boulton and Watt, used to visit Cochrane's father in Scotland.
A512.	Cochrane senior experimented with coal tar; he used to burn off the gas from distillation through metal pipes.
A513.	Blockading Lima.
A514.	All the labourers fled to avoid being conscripted into the rebel army.
A515.	He made a contract with the rebels to carry on.
A516.	The Spanish came back again before he got it signed.
A517.	"Everybody was obliged to fly."
A518.	It was destroyed by both the patriots and the Spanish to keep it out of each other's hands.
A519.	He was conscripted into the army by Bolivar.
A520.	Cast bronze carbines firing nasty expanding (dum-dum) bullets.
A521.	He successfully amputated a labourer's arms.
A522.	He salvaged the frigate *San Martin* in Chorillos Bay, 10 miles from Callao.
A523.	Brass cannon for the owners and a £2,500 fee for himself.
A524.	He used a diving bell.
A525.	Send £2,000 back to Jane at once.

permission to prospect for copper and silver.

Richard Trevithick in Peru

A478. He moved them to Penzance.
A479. Because it was easier for the children to attend school.
A480. He sold off half his patent to William Sims.
A481. His interest in Wheal Francis.
A482. To get a report on the mine from a competent engineer.
A483. It should be anyone but Captain Andrew Vivian.
A484. Income from the plunger-pole engines.
A485. A boiler-maker called James Sanders and the solicitor Richard Page.
A486. He was the lawyer who had drawn up the agreement between Richard Trevithick and Uvillé.
A487. 20th October 1816, in the whaler *Asp*.
A488. February 17th 1817, taking four months. A good passage.
A489. A tumultuous welcome, but engines were in a poor state.
A490. The one in the Mint was making 5 million coins a year (he expected to have it doing 30 million). The two engines at the mines drawing water and the two drawing ore were all in poor state. The rest not even erected.
A491. Henry Vivian died of drink.
A492. It ran through a nunnery.
A493. Abadia could not get permission to enter to inspect and clear it.
A494. He walked up to the nunnery and knocked at the door; he was received very readily.
A495. Ambush and murder.
A496. He was afraid Richard Trevithick would reveal his incompetence and take over.
A497. The gang failed to intercept him.
A498. Uvillé and Page tried to discredit him and take over again.
A499. He walked out on them in 1817.
A500. Abadia, who offered him $8,000 a year.
A501. "On no condition would he consent to deal with these jealousies and ill-treatment".
A502. He used the Viceroy of Lima's (the Marques of Concordia)

A455. 24-inch cylinders, each with 150 feet of 12-inch pumps and 60 feet of 3-inch water pipes.
A456. They had to be capable of disassembly into parts not more than 300lb weight or 7 feet in length.
A457. For transport by mule over the 17000 foot high track to the mines.
A458. 2 feet 6 inches!
A459. Extreme; everything was to be delivered within four months.
A460. Four pumping engines, four winding engines, two crushing mills and four boilers.
A461. A portable engine for use in the Mint in Lima.
A462. £7,000 for the equipment, £1,500 freight charges and £2,300 insurance!
A463. £600.
A464. He offered Richard Trevithick a partnership; £3,000 for a $12,000 share in the company.
A465. One fifth of the profits.
A466. Quite the reverse; he was expressly forbidden.
A467. Thomas Trevarthan, with William Bull as his assistant.
A468. Henry Vivian, husband of Richard Trevithick's younger sister Tamasina.
A469. That Henry was too fond of the bottle.
A470. On September 1st 1814 in the whaler *Wildman*.
A471. John Teague alleged he'd not been paid by Trevithick and Uvillé.
A472. No, they'd given him the £15 which was all they had promised.
A473. January 1815; a very good passage.
A474. February 11th.
A475. As there was no coal they burned wood; Richard Trevithick's instructions on how to do this had been ignored.
A476. Uvillé and his crew were not competent.
A477. To go out himself and take over, which, arguably, he should have done in the first place.

South America

A432. The one between Francisco Uvillé, Don Pedro Abadia and Don José Arismendi.
A433. Uvillé was of Swiss extraction and the two Dons were Spanish merchants.
A434. To bring steam engines and pumps to the drowned silver mines of Cerro de Pasco.
A435. Uvillé came to England and consulted Boulton and Watt.
A436. To forget it! Cerro de Pasco was at an elevation of 14,000 feet and the atmosphere was too thin to work their engines.
A437. A model of Trevithick's high-pressure steam engine.
A438. In the window of Wm Rowley, model maker, 7, Cleveland St., Fitzroy Square, London.
A439. £20.
A440. He took it to the mines and tried it out and found it worked beautifully.
A441. July 11th 1812.
A442. $40,000 (about £8000): 40% for each of the Dons, 20% Uvillé.
A443. To find Trevithick, buy two suitable engines and bring them to Peru.
A444. Up to $30,000 (about £6000).
A445. Two suitable workmen to erect and run the engines and train the local labour.
A446. Offer any sort of partnership to anybody in England.
A447. He fell ill with brain-fever and was landed at Jamaica.
A448. The Falmouth packet *Tilly*.
A449. A cousin by marriage of Richard Trevithick called John Teague.
A450. In Falmouth on May 10th 1813.
A451. Exactly how to find Richard Trevithick.
A452. He was carried ashore still ill to a boarding establishment on Falmouth Moor.
A453. He wrote to Richard Trevithick asking him to come for a meeting.
A454. He had ordered six engines from Rastrick and/or from Pengilly of Neath.

More about John Rastrick

A422. Shropshire, South Wales, Ilfracombe and Cornwall (to meet miners and engineers).
A423. Woolf.
A424. Richard Trevithick's expansion engine.
A425. The breakwater at Plymouth.
A426. A total shambles.
A427. Several ways of improving matters.
A428. He built a rock drilling engine and sold it to the local contractor.
A429. Robert Fox.
A430. Brought them down from 2s 9d to 1s per block.
A431. Richard Trevithick got a share of the savings.

A401. four horses (costing 20s). 15cwt and £63.
A402. Joel Lean's 'Engine Reporter' was the Official Registrar and Recorder of Engine Duty.
A403. In 1811 there were eight engines sized from 36 to 68 inches, averaging 15.7M (9-22 March). In 1813, Richard Trevithick's Wheal Prosper engine, smaller than any of them, recorded 26.7M.
A404. To the Bridgnorth Foundry, working with John Rastrick.
A405. Through Rastrick.
A406. The plunger pole engine.
A407. Wheal Herland.
A408. John Rastrick
A409. Harvey and Vivian in Cornwall, Joseph Price of Neath, etc. who had all missed out on Peru orders.
A410. He spent all of his time working on the Wye Bridge at Chepstow.
A411. The manufacture of the engine was shoddy.
A412. Active sabotage; he ordered the work at Herland to stop.
A413. With his sledgehammer and spanner.
A414. John Rennie, who had advised on the Thames tunnel project.
A415. Captain Anthony Vivian; at risk of being thrown bodily down the mine.
A416. 58 million. Was that a record for a 48in engine?
A417. Matthew Murray put a Richard Trevithick engine into captured French vessel *L'Actif* in Leeds.
A418. A trial run on Breydon Water which was watched by thousands.
A419. *The Experiment* was rechristened *L'Acti,f.*
A420. She began a regular passenger service between Yarmouth and Norwich.
A421. A reckless driver error blew up the boiler in 1816, killing nine people.

Back home

A375. He was declared bankrupt.
A376. He sold his share of the tank patent to Henry Maudsley.
A377. Debts accumulated by the partnership over five years amounted to £4000.
A378. Virtually nothing.
A379. 16 shillings in the pound.
A380. Nothing.
A381. All of Richard Trevithick's assets/property seized and he was made to live in a sponging house.
A382. A house in a street of debtors, between liberty and debtors' prison.
A383. Dickinson had stolen the papers.
A384. The record of depositions to, and proceedings of, the Court!
A385. 1st January 1814.
A386. The first 'Cornish' engine was erected at Wheal Prosper in Gwithian.
A387. An engine working on high pressure steam, working expansively; a condensing engine.
A388. They were the best and most efficient in the world at that time.
A389. The steam was shut off at 1/9th of the stroke.
A390. A 'Cornish' boiler.
A391. Cylindrical boiler with a grate in the end of a tube running the whole length of the boiler. The flue divided at far end to bring flue gases back through boiler under the cylinder and thence to the chimney.
A392. 30ft long, 6ft diameter with a fire tube 3ft 6ins diameter.
A393. 17-18 millions versus 40 millions; the claim to double effectiveness of the old Boulton and Watt machines was therefore valid.
A394. William West at the Hayle Foundry.
A395. A rotative agricultural engine and boiler built 1812.
A396. Sir Christopher Hawkins of Trewithen.
A397. Threshing corn, possibly until 1879.
A398. In the Science Museum.
A399. Lord de Dunstanville of Tehidy.
A400. The machine used 2 bushels of coal (worth 2s 6d) to do the work of

A361. Loss of intellect and brain power.
A362. Dickinson, Jane, and an anonymous letter writer.
A363. Henry Harvey, her brother.
A364. Early September.
A365. He travelled onboard the Falmouth Packet.
A366. His son Richard, aged ten.
A367. Three days in convoy to Dover escorted by gun brig
A368. We were at war with France. Again.
A369. He went ashore for a short walk!
A370. She was chased by French man of war, but escaped.
A371. Six days in all.
A372. Sixteen miles.
A373. They walked!!
A374. His mother had died two months before.

The proposed Reform Tower, pictured against prominent 19th century London landmarks.

The Dickinson disaster

A335. Robert Dickinson, a West Indian merchant.
A336. He was a speculative patent claimer.
A337. 23.
A338. The Nautical Labourer, July 5 1808.
A339. A vessel with a steam engine to move it and load/unload cargo.
A340. Get such a vessel working on the docks, being a fire engine at need.
A341. Regulations banning fires in docks.
A342. Nothing.
A343. Iron tanks for storing liquids on boats.
A344. Manufacture iron tanks
A345. 72, Fore St. Limehouse, London (where Jane and the children were living!).
A346. Carrying liquids, much better than in barrels.
A347. Making the ballasting of ships very cheap indeed (just pump water in or out).
A348. To raise sunken vessels.
A349. Off Margate, in January/February 1810.
A350. Bolted iron tanks to the wreck and pumped them full of air.
A351. Demarcation disputes: the drillers would not put in and tighten bolts and the bolt-tighteners would not drill.
A352. A dispute with its owners about who paid for taking it in.
A353. He cut the ropes and sank it again.
A354. Nothing.
A355. No.
A356. Lack of organisation or system.
A357. File their third patent on April 9.
A358. Iron buoys, iron ships, telescopic masts and yards of iron, floating docks, seasoning timber with warm air, diagonal framing for ships, a rowing trunk propulsion system, steam-cooking galleys, and fresh water from steam condensers.
A359. Iron buoys.
A360. Richard Trevithick collapsed with typhus.

Dredging

A324. General Sir Samuel Bentham.
A325. The boiler explosion at Greenwich.
A326. Three: two x 10hp and one 20hp.
A327. A canal barge, HMS Blazer, and a bombship.
A328. Lifting ballast at 6p/ton.
A329. Worked from boats in open tidal water.
A330. A much bigger engine that would cost £5000.
A331. Made him ask 9p a ton, which was unacceptable.
A332. East and West India Docks dredging clay.
A333. In the estuary dredging mud.
A334. Small high pressure steam engine for driving rock chisels.

The rest of the London adventure: 1802 - 1811

A314. Destroying Napoleon's invasion fleet by steam-driven fire ships.
A315. The Marques of Stafford.
A316. Trentham Hall, Newcastle under Lyme.
A317. Present his ideas to Pitt and Lord Melville.
A318. They kept him waiting for 5 or 6 days and he gave up.
A319. Napoleon moved his army and the panic died down.
A320. He cobbled together a steam-driven boat on a canal.
A321. A sixty to seventy ton barge, with a crankshaft between two flywheels driving two paddles.
A322. It worked well and did about 7mph with paddle wheel tips going at 15mph.
A323. Oliver Evans of Philadelphia.

Catch-me-who-can

A285. A pure locomotive.
A286. One not to be used as a stationary engine but solely for transport.
A287. Making his own rails from wrought iron.
A288. Catch-me-who-can.
A289. At the Hazeldine ironworks under the supervision of John Rastrick.
A290. A cylinder vertical in boiler providing a direct drive to wheels.
A291. To take it to Newmarket to race against any "Mare, horse, or gelding".
A292. Speed. (Oh dear!).
A293. Yes and there was a lot of interest.
A294. To put it on public display on a circular track near Euston Square.
A295. Wooden sleepers as today.
A296. The weight of the engine drove the sleepers into the ground and broke them.
A297. To dig it up and put down foot square blocks as a foundation for the sleepers.
A298. Come and see it and have a ride for a shilling a head.
A299. Mrs. Guilmard, Davies Giddy's sister.
A300. Davies Gilbert.
A301. It was his wife's surname.
A302. President of the Royal Society.
A303. His father Edward was the curate of St Erth church, where Trevithick was married.
A304. Humphrey Davy.
A305. Mechanical Power Subduing Animal Speed.
A306. 12 mph.
A307. 20 mph.
A308. Defray the expenses thus far.
A309. A few weeks.
A310. A rail broke! The engine ran off and turned over.
A311. There were not enough shillings to pay current expenses.
A312. It was installed in a fine old barge once used by the Lord Mayor of London.
A313. None.

A268.	1,040 feet.
A269.	10 or 12 days.
A270.	To seal the weak spot from above using a cofferdam.
A271.	They stopped the work and called in more experts.
A272.	That Richard Trevithick was dead right and the best man for the job
A273.	To call in more experts and, finally, ask anybody for a solution.
A274.	To hold a public competition; they got 54 entries.
A275.	To build the whole tunnel from above using caissons and lay a cast iron tube.
A276.	The whole scheme was abandoned and all the money lost.
A277.	100 years.
A278.	Under the Detroit river and in San Francisco.
A279.	Ten years.
A280.	Another ten years.
A281.	Sir Marc Brunel.
A282.	His son, Isambard Kingdom Brunel.
A283.	Isambard was also nearly killed when the tunnel collapsed.
A284.	72, Fore Street, Limehouse, London.

Trevithick in London

A239. To build a tunnel under the Thames.
A240. Rotherhithe to Limehouse.
A241. The Thames Archway Company.
A242. £1,000: £500 at halfway and another £500 on completion.
A243. 1805.
A244. Robert Vazie.
A245. He was another Cornishman.
A246. His first vertical shaft hit quicksand and the money ran out.
A247. The first year's budget; the company may have had a capital of £140,000!
A248. Davies Giddy, John Rennie and William Chapman.
A249. He pumped Vazie's shaft dry with a steam engine and finished it.
A250. He started the horizontal drift towards the river on August 18.
A251. 188 fathoms or 1128 feet or 376 yards or 344 metres.
A252. 5 feet high, 3 feet wide at the bottom, 2feet 6inches at the top. How did the 6 foot 2 inch, powerfully built, Trevithick deal with it?
A253. A bigger pumping engine, of 30hp.
A254. Vazie was sacked on the 18th.
A255. They had driven 394 feet and were now under the river.
A256. They reached solid rock, which needed hammers and chisels to work.
A257. Gunpowder was far too risky to use just under the river bed.
A258. Jane and the children.
A259. Rotherhithe, address unknown.
A260. Her unopened letters.
A261. 1,028 feet; only 100ft (31m) left to go.
A262. Water flooded in after an unusually high tide and filled the drift. It was very lucky that they all got out.
A263. January 26th.
A264. Richard Trevithick of course.
A265. They tried to discredit Trevithick regarding the quality of his work.
A266. Two colliery managers from the north of England.
A267. Patching and pumping and reinforcing.

A218.	The Navy Board.
A219.	February 21st 1804.
A220.	Ten tons of iron in five wagons with 70 men riding on them.
A221.	Around fifteen tons.
A222.	5 mph.
A223.	4 hours 5 minutes.
A224.	It was necessary to cut down trees and remove rocks to clear the way.
A225.	2cwt.
A226.	A bolt holding the axle to the boiler broke and let all the water out.
A227.	He was completely resigned to the fact that he'd lost the bet.
A228.	They claimed that the return journey was not completed.
A229.	He was injured when his gig overturned.
A230.	The engine was too heavy for the line and kept breaking the plates (rails).
A231.	It worked as a stationary engine for some years.
A232.	Christopher Blackett of Wylam Colliery and built there by John Steel.
A233.	An engineer trained by Richard Trevithick who had employed him at Penydarren.
A234.	It was too heavy for the wooden rails.
A235.	Relaid the track with iron rails.
A236.	1808.
A237.	He'd given up the locomotive business and was engaged in other pursuits.
A238.	George Stephenson and the 2 year old Robert.

The Penydarren locomotive

A189. In 1803.
A190. Samuel Homfray invited him to his Penydarren iron works.
A191. Installing one of his high-pressure engines there.
A192. Four: Dowlais, Plymouth, Cyfartha, and Penydarren.
A193. The Glamorganshire Canal.
A194. To haul their iron down to Cardiff, 24 miles distant.
A195. It was too congested; having 45 locks did not help.
A196. Between Merthyr and Abercynon, nine and a half miles.
A197. An iron railway with a gentle slope of 1 in 145.
A198. Horse-drawn trucks, meaning that it had no cross sleepers.
A199. They were L-shaped in cross-section.
A200. Flanged.
A201. 4 feet 4 inches.
A202. To use a portable engine for factory use and hauling trucks.
A203. Richard Crawshay of Cyfarthfa.
A204. That the smooth wheels would slip.
A205. 500 Guineas that Richard Trevithick could not build a loco to haul 10 tons from Merthyr Tydfil to Abercynon basin on the canal.
A206. To return the empty wagons.
A207. Nine and three-quarters miles.
A208. That was what a single horse could do, one Horse Power!
A209. Richard Hill of the Plymouth Works.
A210. In Homfray's factory.
A211. Cast-iron with wrought iron return flue, with the firebox next to the chimney.
A212. Into the chimney, three feet above the boiler.
A213. $8^{1}/_{4}$ inches diameter, 54 inch stroke, set in the boiler above the flue.
A214. From a crosshead through gears to left-hand wheels and a large flywheel.
A215. It was intended as a stationary engine too,
A216. To overcome top dead centre problem, essential on a stationary engine.
A217. Simon Goodrich.

More about 1802-1804: trains

A173. Up to 150 pounds per square inch.
A174. At Coalbrookdale in August 1802.
A175. A railway locomotive.
A176. W.A. Reynolds.
A177. He had toyed with the idea of building a steam locomotive.
A178. That the world's first locomotive ran on rails at Coalbrookdale in 1803.
A179. There is no other record of it, and no mention of it when Penydarren hit the headlines.
A180. A boiler explosion at Greenwich.
A181. September 8th 1803.
A182. Three killed and one seriously injured.
A183. 6 feet diameter with walls 1inch thick.
A184. Over 100 yards and 500lbs.
A185. The boy looking after the engine went away to catch eels.
A186. The labourer he left in charge saw it racing and half turned it off.
A187. A second safety valve and a fusible plug.
A188. The incident was exploited Boulton and Watt, not just his competitors but also the promoters of the low-pressure engine; they highlighted the perceived risks of using high pressure steam

The next step - London!

A148. To patent the high-pressure engines.
A149. For stationary or locomotive use.
A150. Richard Trevithick, Andrew Vivian, (40% each) and William West (20%)
A151. Davies Giddy and Lord de Dunstanville.
A152. Humphrey Davy and Count Rumford.
A153. 26th March 1802.
A154. Steam exhausted through the chimney!
A155. It was more like a stage-coach.
A156. By West at Harvey's in Hayle.
A157. William Felton's coach-building works Leather Lane, Clerkenwell.
A158. Big enough for eight inside passengers.
A159. Two 8 foot driving wheels at back; one tiller-controlled steering wheel at front.
A160. The firebox design – the fire bars worked loose and dropped coals into ash-pan.
A161. Usually 5-6 mph but could go comfortably at 8-9 mph.
A162. It was on the flat.
A163. Left a great deal to be desired.
A164. Tottenham Court Road, Euston Square, mostly.
A165. Oxford Street; it had been cleared of horses and carriages and the shops were closed.
A166. Mr Trevithick's Dragon.
A167. Not one.
A168. In a hoop rolling mill, where it worked well for many years.
A169. Rough riding and poor steering, which plagued such vehicles for many years.
A170. There was no differential gear, it could only drive one or other of rear wheels, not both.
A171. None, really.
A172. They were frightened by it.

A137. To form a partnership to develop the engine and to show it off to the gentry: Giddy, de Dunstanville, and the Vivian family.
A138. Richard Trevithick and Andrew Vivian set off 28 Dec to go the two miles to Tehidy, the de Dunstanville home. Andrew steered it into a gully, lost control, and it overturned.
A139. The very first road traffic accident to a powered vehicle!
A140. They pushed it into a building and went to a pub, forgetting to put out the fire. The boiler boiled dry, got red-hot, and set fire to the contraption.
A141. £70.
A142. The "Puffing Devil".
A143. The road journey was repeated by a replica built by the Trevithick Society.
A144. A Trevithick engine grinding corn.
A145. That the design of the boiler with a flat end made it a death trap.
A146. "Made of a round figure, to bear the expansive action of steam".
A147. In one piece.

The Camborne Road Carriage

A112. Nicholas-Joseph Cugnot. Paris, 1769-70.
A113. water ran out after only 20 minutes, it was not possible to add water to the boiler without cooling it right down and the steering was so atrocious that the vehicle probably crashed on its trial run
A114. Abandoned and forgotten.
A115. William Murdoch.
A116. Boulton and Watt.
A117. They did not think it would work but if it did they wanted a share of the profit.
A118. Four.
A119. At the Budge Foundry.
A120. Richard Trevithick and Captain Andrew Vivian.
A121. The use of high-pressure steam.
A122. Boulton and Watt made it plain that they would oppose the patent. He chose to keep his safe comfortable job rather than fight for a project which might never make a penny.
A123. He never made a full-size working steam carriage.
A124. He invented gas lighting
A125. Whether or not smooth wheels would grip the road or skid?
A126. He hired a one-horse chaise and went out in it with Davies Giddy; they forced the wheels round on hills by hand and it climbed.
A127. James Watt when he first came into Cornwall.
A128. Harvey's Foundry at Hayle.
A129. Local blacksmith Jonathan Tyack.
A130. At Tyack's blacksmith's shop at the Weeth in Camborne.
A131. Richard Trevithick's cousin Captain Andrew Vivian.
A132. Late in the day of Christmas Eve 1801.
A133. Up to the top of Beacon Hill in Camborne Hill and back.
A134. Down Tehidy Road; the road up Beacon Hill had not been built at that time.
A135. "We jumped on, 7 or 8 of us. It was a stiffish hill, (1 in 20) but she went off like a little bird."
A136. "Faster than I could walk".

A98. Ding Dong Mine in 1798/9.
A99. At least 14.
A100. 350 guineas.
A101. A trial against their engines.
A102. Dolcoath Mine.
A103. £50.
A104. Benjamin Glanville.
A105. Burying coal for unrecorded use.
A106. By fitting a short piston.
A107. Over 3 or 4 days, with invigilators recording the amount of coal burnt and the number of kibbles raised.
A108. "She beat Boulton and Watt all to nothing".
A109. A puffer mounted on wheels; a vehicle.
A110. Boulton and Watt's patents expired (after 30 years!)
A111. John Holman's, later Holman Brothers.

The commemorative placque in Basset Road, Camborne, the location of the Christmas Eve run of the Puffing Devil.

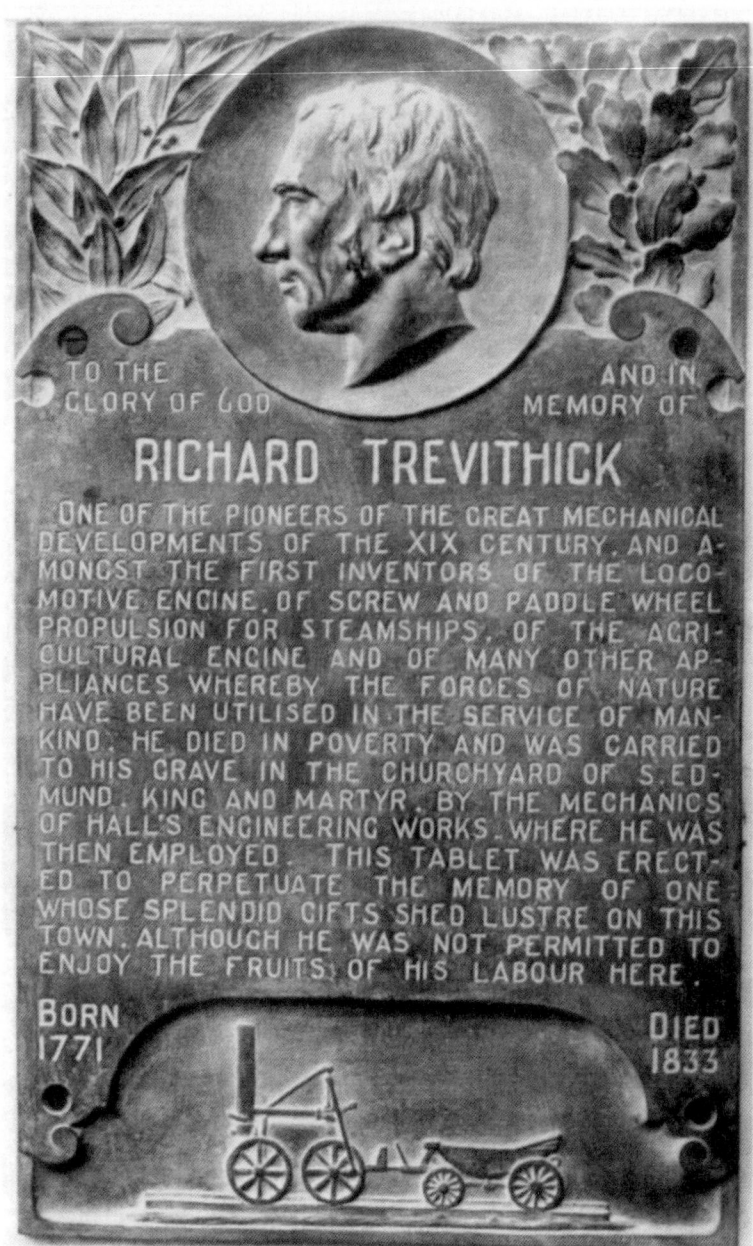

The commemorative placque in Dartford church yard, Trevithick's final resting place.

Adult Trevithick

A67. His father died on August 1st.
A68. Richard had to take over all his responsibilities.
A69. Mine captain at Dolcoath, Wheal Treasury, Eastern Stray Park and Wheal Chance.
A70. Agent to the Bassett (Lord de Dunstanville's) family.

A71. He married Jane Harvey (sister of Joanna; see question 65).
A72. November 7th at St Erth Parish Church.
A73. Moreton House in Redruth.
A74. The Trevithick House in Penponds, near Camborne. 1798.
A75. Took the key to Redruth house with him and incurred a year's rent.
A76. Richard Trevithick (III).
A77. Steam-powered plunger pumps.
A78. Only on ones he installed himself; this was not patentable.
A79. The water-powered plunger engine.
A80. Prince William Harry Mine at Roskear in 1798.
A81. There was not enough water.
A82. At the Alport lead mines in Derbyshire and at Coalbrookdale.
A83. Nothing.
A84. Cook's Kitchen Mine in 1799.
A85. Hauling up ore; replacing a horse whim.
A86. Small high-pressure engines for winding etc, in mines.
A87. Dolcoath Mine.
A88. A steam condenser was not necessary.
A89. Davies Giddy's.
A90. That the loss of steam would only be one atmosphere.
A91. In his kitchen.
A92. William West.
A93. Davies Giddy.
A94. Lady De Dunstanville.
A95. 50 pounds pre square inch.
A96. Through a blast-pipe into the chimney.
A97. Put a water jacket round it to preheat the water.

A63. William West.
A64. Harvey's of Hayle.
A65. He married Joanna Harvey in 1784.
A66. Models of strong steam locomotive and stationary engines.

The new commemorative placque at the Bull Inn, Dartford.

A29.	Wrestling.
A30.	Richard Hodge.
A31.	Dinner in the Dolcoath count house. The building was kept up with its ceiling as memorial.
A32.	56 lbs.
A33.	A sledge hammer!
A34.	A pump barrel.
A35.	Seven or eight hundredweight.
A36.	A smith's mandrel weighing 10cwt, now in the Science Museum.
A37.	Davies Giddy.
A38.	A member of College of Surgeons.
A39.	That he had never seen such a well-developed physique.
A40.	By going round mines and looking at the engines, talking to the men who used them and the men who had built them.
A41.	A large copper deposit discovered in Anglesey.
A42.	Parys mountain.
A43.	They were flooding the market with copper cheaper than could be produced in Cornwall.
A44.	They did not cover strong steam.
A45.	High-pressure steam; steam at over two atmospheres pressure.
A46.	He did not think it was safe.
A47.	Jonathan Hornblower of Penryn.
A48.	A compound engine feeding used steam from one cylinder to another cylinder.
A49.	Davies Giddy.
A50.	Tincroft Mine in 1791.
A51.	Dolcoath Mine in 1786, aged 15.
A52.	Engineer at East Stray Park Mine in March 1791, aged 19.
A53.	24s to 26s to 30s a month.
A54.	His father and uncle as captains (at £2 per month each) and cousin John.
A55.	Aged 21 he was engaged to test the Hornblower engine at Tincroft Mine.
A56.	That it was not significantly better than a Boulton and Watt engine.
A57.	Edward (Ned) Bull.
A58.	Boulton and Watt won their case against him in 1792.
A59.	Ding Dong Mine in 1796.
A60.	Bailiffs trying to serve injunctions upon them.
A61.	In Birmingham, while visiting Boulton and Watt's Soho factory!
A62.	Wheal Treasury.

Young Trevithick

A1.	13 April 1771.
A2.	What is now 35 Station Road, Pool, Illogan.
A3.	1760.
A4.	They were both mine captains.
A5.	Anne Teague.
A6.	Ireland.
A7.	Penponds, near Camborne.
A8.	Trevithick Cottage is now owned by the National Trust and was previously owned by the Trevithick Society.
A9.	Tamesin or Thomasina
A10.	The Newcomen engine, erected at Dolcoath Mine
A11.	A new deep adit
A12.	Boulton and Watt moved into Cornwall
A13.	Watt's patent feature, the separate steam condenser.
A14.	From between 25% to 33%.
A15.	It was possible to mine more than twice as deep as with a Newcomen engine.
A16.	12 years; from 1778 to 1790.
A17.	Coal (for engine boilers) does not occur in Cornwall and had to be shipped in from Wales; it was therefore expensive.
A18.	One-third the saving in fuel costs.
A19.	Boulton and Watt!
A20.	Made his model steam locomotive.
A21.	Boulton and Watt discouraged him, seeing no advantage in the idea.
A22.	He needed their patents and he worked for them.
A23.	He invented gas lighting and died rich!
A24.	Disastrously; the teacher couldn't stand him.
A25.	"A disobedient, slow, obstinate spoiled boy, frequently absent and very inattentive."
A26.	Six.
A27.	Sport and games.
A28.	Six feet 2 inches in his stockinged feet.